IN SEARCH OF LIGHT IN THE DARKNESS

Contemporary Thoughts of Manipur at the Beginning of New Millennium

IN SEARCH OF LIGHT IN THE DARKNESS

Contemporary Thoughts of Manipur at the Beginning of New Millennium

H. Ramananda Singh

AKANSHA PUBLISHING HOUSE
NEW DELHI • GUWAHATI • VISAKHAPATNAM

AKANSHA PUBLISHING HOUSE
4649-B/21, Ansari Road
Daryaganj, New Delhi-110002
Phones: 23268193, 09435116718
Email: ektabooks@yahoo.com
visit us: www.akanshapublishinghouse.com

In Search of Light in the Darkness

First Published 2011

ISBN 978-81-8370-278-2

PRINTED IN INDIA

Published by Akansha Publishing House, New Delhi-110002 and printed at Harmain Offset Printers, Delhi.

Dedicated

to

my father

H. Komol Singh

Contents

Foreword

As responsible citizens of our country we cannot remain indifferent to the socio-political and historical events around. For whatever might happen, these have a lasting impression on our psyche. We try to comprehend the reasons and impact of various occurrences in our own way. In fact none can deny that indifference is a deadly virus that jeopardizes whatever we might have inherited from the civilization. Sometimes there are enough reasons to feel despondent about the chain of events on which, as individual citizens, we have no control. Nevertheless we try to decipher the nuances of the turmoils which engulf us from all quarters.

That is why, in spite of his busy schedule as an academician, Dr. H. Ramananda Singh has embarked upon the search of light in the midst of darkness in the Eastern most province of Manipur. His genuine feelings emanating from both existential and cultural crisis have found eloquent expression in this well executed monograph. Even a cursory look at the table of contents will set at rest any question with regards to the intention of the author. His style is lucid and transparent. That is why, the expected communication with the readers is established in no time.

Since the author is a faculty member of a University Management Studies Department, he talks about spectre of mismanagement of Chief Executive Officer and tries to relate his direct experiences at Manipur with the task of building up an efficient as well as effective management system in the midst of confusion and unrest in the society around. The author exhibits rare capacity to blend subjectivity and objectivity in his discourse. At time he is philosophical while basically his stance is that of a seasoned social scientist.

I am sure the readers would find this monograph interesting and have a glimpse of Manipur in turmoils at the juncture of the new millennium. I recommend this monograph to the reader community and hope that they will not hesitate to offer their patronage to this intriguing discourse.

(Prof. Tapodhir Bhattacharjee)

Vice-Chancellor
ASSAM UNIVERSITY
Silchar - 788 011, Assam.

Acknowledgements

Conceiving and bringing out a book of this nature requires the contribution of many people. I cannot in full measure, reciprocate the encouragement given, the inspiration showered and the contribution made by various persons in my endeavour to complete this book.

I must, however, specially acknowledge my indebtedness to Prof. Tapodhir Bhattacharjee, the Vice-Chancellor of Assam University, an erudite scholar himself, who's scholarly and literary words have been a source of my inspiration in the field of literature.

I shall also remain grateful to Prof. Apurbananda Mazumdar and Prof. R.K. Raul of Department of Management Studies, Assam University, Who were sources of continuous guidance and inspiration to me, not only, as a person, but also, as a teacher.

I also would like to thank Dr. Gurudas Das, Head, Department of Humanities, NIT,

Silchar, who always extend his help and guidance to me as a brother.

I would also like to thank two of my friends Kh. Premananda Singh and S. Samarendra Singh who always stand with me through ups and downs in my life.

Finally, for whatever I have become and all that I have accomplished, I owe a special debt to my parents, my wife and my son Aditya. Without their love and support, I would not have made it to where I am today.

H. Ramananda Singh

Preface

This book entitled "In Search of Light in the Darkness" is an anthology of collected small articles which were written at the beginning of this century during my stay in Manipur as a teacher while serving Manipur University.

I was perplexed to find the socioeconomic and political conditions of Manipur totally different from what I used to know and experienced as a young boy before I left Manipur in the year 1986 for higher studies.

The patriotic feeling I had and the pride of being a citizen of Manipur was hurt. Nothing could be done, except sharing my concerns about the future of Manipur with my friends, colleagues and students. Occasionally I used to vent out my anxieties about the state of affairs of the state through the esteemed newspaper of the state "*The Imphal Free Press*".

It is high time that we think, share thoughts, discuss and do whatever we are supposed to do for Manipur for the well-being of her future where we can have a sound good night sleep without the slightest shadow of any anxiety and worries.

In the November month of 2004, a few students of Assam University came to Manipur University for participating in the inter-University youth festival. As they wanted to see Loktak Lake, I took them to Shendra, Moirang, but had to return without seeing the beauty of the lake from the top of the Shendra hill, for we need to get the permission from the army authority which we never knew of its existence earlier.

For seeing the beauty of our own land or showing it to somebody, when we require to take the permission, indicating that we cannot even move freely in our own homeland, whose pride will be hurt if not ours?

This book appeals to whosoever have a concern and feel for the Manipur and its people to take the initiative of sharing ideas and thoughts for taking us to the path of prosperity and bringing glory to Manipur.

This small piece of book has been born out of my concern for the future generations as to what type of society they will be inheriting from us, if the present situations of daily bloodshed, misunderstanding, priority to self, and lack of transparency in the administration continue.

This book is not going to serve for everyone. It is for those who not only have a deep rooted concern for the people, but also the courage to take a stand for a cause.

H. Ramananda Singh

Map of Manipur

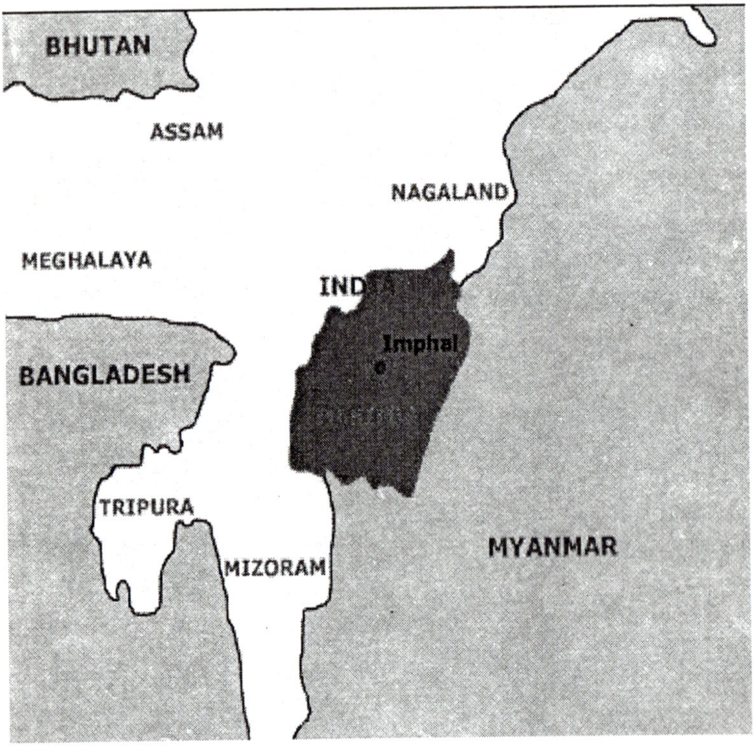

Manipur state is situated in the North-Eastern corner of India.

1 Who is to be Blamed!

14th Feb, 2000
Manipur

It was a calm night of April '99, before the starting of that year's long awaited monsoon. While walking on a deserted road amidst the well appreciated corrupt environments ridden with daily bloodshed, a voice of a dejected youth was heard shouting aloud breaking the silence of the night. The voice thundered "If at all to be blamed for what's happening in today's society, blame it on schools and colleges that have given us degrees and certificates but have failed to produce good citizens for a better tomorrow."

My mind did wonder what has gone wrong with today's education system. I also recalled an article where it was mentioned that the purpose of national education policy is to produce good citizens. I wonder whether an educated youth blaming the school and colleges that have given degrees and certificates as a symbol of a good citizen of the country.

I also wonder whether the learning youths, who are the pillars of the future society, breaking the furniture, torching school buildings and govt. departments built by public money while expressing their grievances are also in the process of becoming a good citizen.

I wonder whether some teachers while telling the students whether they take classes or not they will be getting the salary from the govt., sending the message that whether one does one's duty or not, it hardly matters, is also a way of imparting education to make good citizens. It seems our intellectuals and learned teachers have an illusive belief that govt. has money plants in the assembly that can be plucked whenever needed. They might have ignored the fact that every individuals in different walks of life are contributing to their salary with the expectations that their children can get some values from the teachers.

But why to blame only the schools and the colleges where students are there only for a few hours in a day, while the youths are being educated by different institutions of the society having different conflicting objectives. The family institution, regulatory institution, religious and political institutions are playing important roles in transforming our youths.

Some of the parents in the family institution might also be indirectly helping the education system in its present state by promoting their wards to copy during their examination either directly or indirectly with the help of hired teachers.

I wonder where are they heading the tender youths to? Are they not inculcating in them the skill of self-deception and deceiving other?

Men in regulatory institution are also seen faithfully playing their role in this regard, beating innocents in the public places seems to be the best way to make the youths recognise their place in the society. What a nice educational strategy?

People's representatives or custodian of the societal reforms are also not lagging behind. With a meaningful smile, Mahatma Gandhi and his preachings are maximally used as a tool of election campaign. After elections are over they are lost in the hectic program of serving the society through more extraction and least of contribution approach. After all they have invested a lot in the form of 500 rupees currency notes promptly displaying the father of the nations. May be, the soul of Mahatma feels like crying.

Nevertheless, the formal education system has been focussing too much on hardware aspect i.e. higher marks and certificates. It has ignored the critical elements (software aspects) of inputs to instil values that make good citizens. Inculcation of the belief that today's youth should shoulder the responsibility of shifting "I" to "We" and of expanding the horizon "we" beyond the boundaries of individual family, community and religion, i.e. "we" for all and "we" for a nation should be given the first priority.

Amazingly, we have been waiting for a quite long time for the environment where we can have a sound good night's sleep without anxiety. Moreover when every responsible individual are not doing what they are supposed to do, **whom should we blame?**

2. Death of an Idea!

14th Feb, 2000
Manipur

On one of the hot Saturday nights of Bombay, 1995, while the others were having a cheerful journey along the waves of imagination towards their respective dream world, two of my friends and I were haunting for an idea amidst the murky jungle of ignorance and complexity through a rigorous brain storming session.

Gone were the days when we got the opportunity of listening to the views and ideas of intellectuals and the learned members of the society. It seemed they have resolved to confine themselves and their valuable ideas within the four walls of high raised buildings that were enveloped by the cloud of fear.

Moreover, their valuable ideas and views were never implemented either by them or by other.

To fill in the vacuum created by the intellectuals of the society, we volunteered ourselves to shoulder the responsibility of hunting for the new ideas for the well being of the society.

So, our idle and hazy minds set out hunting for an innovative idea on one Saturday night while all citizens fell into a sound good night's sleep after they had a hectic schedule of the week without having any anxiety for the next day (Sunday).

In search for an idea, our undeterred but exhausted minds went deeper and deeper into the jungle of ignorance along with the thunder of agreement and disagreement among us.

Along the painful journey some insignificant ideas were seen lurking here and there but the good ideas had been eluding the focus of our imagination.

At last, at a near distance not far from us, behind a thorny bush we saw the illumination of a good idea. Indeed, great were the pains we had undertaken before we got the idea.

At the beginning of our discussion, we wondered what would be the future of our country run by democratic govt., when its people no longer have belief (in the true sense of the term) in democracy.

Moreover, emotions and feelings of the people

are crushed by the conflicting goals of so many governments (political government, police government, military government, underworld government, revolutionary government etc.) that rule the people at the same time.

Political leaders seem to have forgotten the fact that the restoration of the faith of the people in democracy is more important than that of ruling over them.

Among the people who suffer most is the poor. We thought of taking the initiative to restore the faith of the poor people by reducing their burden through our innovative ideas.

In winter, the poor have no woollen clothes to protect their body from the spectre of the piercing cold waves that devour them.

And in summer, since they cannot afford electricity not to speak of fans and air conditioners, they cannot protect their skins from the elongated fiery tongue of the scorching heat of the sun that licks their body and sucks the soul out of it.

Keeping the sufferings of the people in the mind, we wanted to manufacture a tablet, which could maintain the human body at room temperature.

If that happens even the Eskimos may not need woollen clothes and the people living in the tropical countries may not need fans and air conditioners. In fact, inventing the tablet was a good idea and we were not bothered much about the feasibility of its implementation.

But something did bother us. If the people both poor and rich started buying our tablets, what would happen to the woollen and fan/A.C industries? The companies would close, many people would be rendered jobless and there would be chaos in the socio-economic conditions of the country.

The owners of the companies would be fuming with anger and would give SUPARI in our names to contract killers. We indeed foresaw so many problems.

Finally, we decided to kill our unique idea and throw the dead idea into the sea after it was wrapped in a hanky.

And today, like the remains of the unsinkable Titanic, our idea is lying there under the seabed waiting for someone to put life into it.

But we still wonder, whether an imagination that can never be implemented can be called an idea?

3 Deceiving Smiles!

In the year 2000
Manipur.

A good looking Mr. Amrit once told me, with a smile, why I was always wearing a serious face. Further, he told me that nothing would cost me in smiling.

As a person who never accepted defeat without having been defeated, I had to defend myself. As a defensive device I retorted, with a distorted face by pulling my face while trying to smile, by saying that deep within my heart I was smiling and if the God given face appeared seriousness to his eyes, I was not to be blamed for.

By pulling a little pressure on my mind, I tried to recall any incident when I had tried to bring smile on my face and if any productive result that I got out of it and also the cost associated with the smile.

When I was in seventh standard, a stoutly built Gorilla like my class fellow used to batter me everyday. In fact, he was using muscle power and not political power to make me knew that he was a superior species.

I used to tell him, with an innocent smile, not to be so rude to a class fellow. Unfortunately, the more there was smile on my face the more he beat me. But the *channa* for 50 paise that I offered him everyday (like the food and a man offered to the demon *Bokasur* of the Mahabharata) did what my smile could not have done.

Had the vigilant officer known about it, my gorilla friend and I might have been booked for corruption?

Another incident also came to my mind. Not a many days ago, one of my friends and I were returning from the market. On the way, few personnel in uniform were checking every passer-by and a few youths were also seen sunning themselves (youths picked up by the police and parading for interrogation and identification) under the scorching heat with hands raised.

When we reached near the checking, I pulled my face reluctantly and smiled at the personnel. Fortunately, we were allowed to go without checking and I was very happy and at the thought that, at last, my smile got a productive result.

Amazingly, my happiness was short lived as the event turned out to be cause of my embarrassment when my younger brother told me that it was not for my smile but my bulging tummy for which we were allowed to go without checking, for they (personnel) knew we could not be the one (underground activists) whom they are looking for.

Here also, perhaps, something had done what my smile could not have done.

I also remembered an officer who occupied a responsible position with the dignified responsibilities. All the files and bills were required to be routed through him just because his signature was required for further processing of the file.

Whenever people came to him enquiring about their files, he always smiled back while telling it would be processed as soon as possible. But what the people got was repeated assurance and deceiving smiles. Whether the officer was waiting for some tangibility or he did not have the mental ability to take decision or his watchdog did not have time to advise him was not known to me.

If one ever wished to enumerate the cost of his deceiving smiles, one had to count the number of wrinkles or lines (created by the artificial smile) coming up on his forehead that made him look older than the actual age. That was the explicit cost and the implicit cost was the loss of faith bestowed upon him by the people.

Also, the stories of deceiving smiles from beautiful girls causing nightmares in the life of their admirers were also not uncommon.

Verily, deceiving smile is a smile, which never is a true smile.

In an article, it was mentioned that in Russia after the opening up of its closed economy and when privatisation just started, employer of a big shop gave 4 extra rubbles to his employees for every smile they made on the customers. Those smiles were not the deceiving smiles but the smiles to make the customers comfortable and feel at home.

Nevertheless, we believe, smile is the manifestation of a good soul that smoothens and enlightens the onlookers. A true smile should be from the heart of heart, without any expectations from the receiver (if so, it may amount to corruption through smile), emanating the warm feelings of the brotherhood and friendship.

In spite of this belief, can we afford to have a true smile without remaining indifferent to whatever that is happening around us?

4 Mathematical Interpretation of Complex Culture

21st June, 2000.
Manipur.

A handsome boy clad in jeans with rolled up sleeves, wearing an earring on the left side of his ear lobe and having a long untrimmed hair tied with a rubber band, once asked me, "What is Complex culture?"

To a person having Mathematical background, it was a thought provoking question but difficult to give an answer.

Without much of thinking, I told him, if a societal setup, which is intertwined with unprecedented behaviours, has no unique identity of its own, in which every happening is not cleared (as to what it is, and why it is) and the members of the society are not sure about the type of beliefs and the values to be handed down to the future generation, then the society is said to be beset with complex culture.

The boy seemed to be satisfied with my illogical answer but the very question took me to my wonderland hunting for the right answer.

Amidst the lack of agreement as to what we mean by the term Culture, I groped my way in search of light in the darkness.

Amazingly, to some, stones, axes, pottery, and bowls are culture. To some, culture is behaviour. And some have the notion that culture is a set of values, beliefs, and behaviour pattern that form the core identity of a society.

But to the Mathematician, culture consists of 'n' different social signals correlated with 'm' different responses.

As a child grows up into man, he grows up amidst different social signals that interact with his inner psyche. He learns by observing whatever that is happening around him and forms the belief system of his own as to what is good and bad. Belief system leads to the formation of attitude, which is the pre-disposition of action tendencies, and finally expresses it into responses (behaviour).

In short, behaviour is the response, governed by the belief system, to whatever the signals we get from the surroundings.

So, culture is behaviour (responses). Custom and law that nurture the value system of the society play very important roles during the growing age of a child in the formation of his belief system, which selects the signals and ultimately pass the selected signals into the inner psyche of the child. If the law and the custom, guided by the societal values for maintaining the values, are perfect, those signals that are detrimental to the society will never be selected by the belief system of the child.

Hence, the belief and the value systems, from the detrimental and unacceptable signals, protect the child.

Further, beliefs can be divided into core beliefs and secondary beliefs. The people living in a particular society hold many core beliefs and values that tend to persist.

Most American still believe in work, in getting married, in giving to charity, and in being honest. Core beliefs and values are passed on from parent to their children and are enforced by major social institutions –schools, religious gathering and Govt.

Secondary beliefs and values are opened to change. Believing in work is core belief, believing that people ought to get extra money apart from salary for doing work such as processing of a file is secondary belief. Although core beliefs are fairly persistent, cultural swings do take place through secondary beliefs and values with time. In 1960s of America, the advent of hippies, the Beatles, Elvis Presley, and other cultural phenomenon had a major impact on young people's hairstyle, clothing, sexual norms, and life goals. Today's young people are influence by new heroes and fads.

To be precise, if the secondary beliefs and values are stronger than the core beliefs and values, it will overshadow the core beliefs and existing culture will be changed entirely.

A boy wearing an earring may be a temporary phenomenon, which is influenced by the secondary belief. It may be either a fad emulating other or an expression of daring personality, which enable him to get recognition from his colleagues. However, on second thought: on one side the boy, by wearing an earring instead of two, may be lessening the economic burden of his parents in particular and society in general, the economy of which depends upon the salary of a few government employees (if the salary of the govt. employees get delayed, the economy of the state remained stand still), and on the other he may be keeping the old tradition of wearing earrings alive.

Nevertheless, I sometimes wonder what the future anthropologists would interpret if any remains of the bodies of the youths who are untraceable in the missing culture (often youths got disappeared and untraceable as result of which there were protests and general strikes blaming the govt. and charging the paramilitary forces responsible by the general public) of today were extricated. With great dismay, using their superb analytical skills, they may shockingly conclude that the culture of late twentieth and early twenty first century as primitive wearing an earring on one side of the ear(defying the nature's established norms of symmetry)and also had the culture of making a hole in the head(with bullet!)(General public have the suspicion that youths were picked up by the army and killed them).

While believing, culture is handed down or inherited from the earlier generations, we also know that that the certain behaviours of the present society were not familiar with earlier generations. This suggests that some signals apart from our own social signals are also creeping into the society and are instrumental in changing gradually the core beliefs that form the culture of the society.

A myriad of cultures, beaming from the sky through satellite channels, reaches every house and educates the learning and receptive minds that discern useful and unuseful signals. And a few privilege people, who got the opportunity for real interactions with the polished culture of the developed society, brought home a refined real culture along with them by enriching their core beliefs.

But to some fancy minds, which are yet to develop a psychological resistance to abusive signals (violence, easy going, exploitation, abusive behaviour, etc.) but having the illusive beliefs that these signals represent an ideal culture of the developed society, certain signals turn into an imaginary culture.

Since secondary beliefs and values are open to change, to some it may change into illusive beliefs leading to an imaginary culture.

People talk about modernised African culture, which is the outcome of the interaction of the real polished European culture and the traditional African culture.

But what will be the outcome when our real culture interacts with an imaginary culture?

If an individual culture, which shaped by the societal real culture, interacts admiringly with and imaginary culture, it may lead to an individual complex culture. However it cannot lead to complex culture of the society so long as other members of the society do not blindly emulate the imaginary culture.

Moreover, culture may also be regarded as a system consisting of knowledge, belief, art, moral, law, custom and any other capabilities and habits acquired by man as the member of the society.

This element of culture, by interacting and correlating with one another, form a unique core identity of the society. And if there is no proper relationship among its elements, the system changes into a complex system (complex culture) and the original system loses its identity. Thus the complex culture is produced either by the responses governed by the illusive beliefs that cannibalised the core beliefs and values or by the imbalance relationship among the elements of the culture.

Sometimes certain complex behaviour of an individual or a small group of individuals slowly diffuse into the society, quite unknown to its members. People realised only after it has become a part of the societal culture and when nothing can be done to stop its venom.

When the corruption has become a culture percolating down to different strata of the society, can we bring a full stop (.) to corruption?

The daily bloodshed among fellow brethren and the regular missing of youths, before these happenings culminate into the culture, is not a high time we brought an end to it?

While dwelling amidst the complexity of the socio-economic and political environment, the crucial need of the hour that we see today is a psychological revolution for bringing a change in our mindset to enrich the core beliefs and values.

A psychological revolution will bring about a cohesive and conducive behaviour in the society for a better tomorrow, where our future generation will feel proud to inherit a rich culture from us.

Having a culture that gives us prosperous and meaningful life without any element of complexity, will it ever remain as a dream wrapped in a mystery?

5 The Haunting Ghost of Fear!

13th March, 2000

Manipur.

A few days back, we happened to call on a sick friend at his residence. It seemed our friend has stepped into a new millennium by riding high fever.

It was in the evening of the first week of January 2000. Hardly had we sat down enquiring about the health of the sick friend, the good father of our friend was telling us to go before it was late. The concerned father was murmuring something, though not completely audible. He uttered, "Time has changed and it has become unsafe to go out after the dusk".

Indeed, things have changed a lot. A small voice in me keeps asking whether people and the direction of their thinking also have changed not for the sake of the need of a change but a change out of fear.

By stopping the wheels of the clock, my mind

wanders back to the mid '70s when life used to be so peaceful.

In those days, society was closely knitted by the bond of concern for fellow friends through high interaction. We had meaningful night life though in a small way, yet contributing a lot in nurturing social cohesiveness.

People after hectic schedule during the day found some leisure time in the evening for relaxing their tired minds with various programs that helped them to laugh away all the worries. Whenever a child was born to a family, there were *dramas*, music, etc. on the night of the *swasti puja*. Those programs were in fact, the mirror as well as the heritage of our own society and indirectly responsible for bringing social harmony to some extend. Sometimes, in the middle of the night, people called on sick friends and relatives with dimly lit lanterns in their hands.

As a kid we also enjoyed the stories of *Mahabharata* and *Ramayana* along with the elders during the summer nights from pillow beating professional story teller (as and when the story teller wanted to give emphasis to some point or to draw the attention of the audiences he used to beat the pillow on his lap with a loud sound by his right hand). Everyday, after dinner, we used to have a short distance walk before retiring. Life had been peaceful and there was not much of a social tension.

Unfortunately today, nobody dares to venture out at night. People prefer to remain indoors and within their own domains.

Even the stray dogs no longer loiter in the street for fear of meeting the hunting boots (of Army) and the strayed bullets. Even inside the four walls of the house 100% safety is not guaranteed, for if any untoward accident happens nearby, the horrible scene of Jallianwala Bagh Massacre may be repeated (if any bomb blast or gun shots occurred, the nearby innocent civilians were mowed down in retaliation by the security forces).

Eventually, after experiencing with all the happening around, some people have professed adaptability and started adapting themselves to the environment which they do not belong to. It seems that they have resigned themselves to the fate and allowed the ghost of fear to haunt them in their inner psyche.

Instead of changing it, shall we adapt or adjust to the environment which suffocates not only few but the majority of us?

After, so said, 50 years of the Independence, still we are living in fear in our own native land.

It is worth pondering, from whom we really are afraid of? Is it from our own native brethren or from some alien?

The ghost of fear is more fearsome than the fear itself as it torments free thinking process with regimentation. What else one can think of, except submitting oneself reluctantly to whatever is being imposed, when the horizon of one's mind is enveloped with fear and haunted by its ghost.

Should we not stop for a while to introspect if being haunted and hunted is our destiny and destination?

6 The Spectre of Mismanagement of a Chief Executive Officer

13th April 2000

Manipur

As we step into 21st century, and with the era of networking and internet gathering momentum, and the people demanding more of transparency, I had a belief that our CEO might not have tried to cross the LOC that separates 2nd and 3rd millennium.

But to my great dismay, my belief deceives me like no other the CEO not only has stepped into the new millennium (after winning election) but also has strengthened its position in the mind of the people with a unique selling proposition (USP) which sloganeered, "the CEO that identifies with your culture."

Surprisingly, the magic of the CEO is such that not a single day passes without a single word being heard about him with allusive to his Mismanagement of the affairs of the state. People write about and talk about Mismanagement without giving any clue as to what leads to Mismanagement.

It seems the CEO and the spectre of his Mismanagement has come here to stay forever by making its presence felt in all subsystems of personalised governance in our democratic set-up.

My mind wonders how our CEO charms the people and how the spectre of his Mismanagement has crept into our own way of life.

But the little knowledge that I have could not throw any light to remove the darkness of my doubt about our CEO and his Mismanagement.

Nevertheless, those who are at the helm of affairs might have invited the spectre of Mismanagement whenever they missed the critical elements that make a sound management.

As a matter of fact, management emphasises effectiveness and efficiency of the things we do. Effectiveness refers to doing the right things and efficiency refers to doing the things right. According to Bill Clinton, the president of USA, doing the right things is economics.

Moreover, identification of the things to be done on the priority basis and maximum utilisation of inputs for maximum output are the critical elements of a sound management leading to economic development.

But the choice of the things to which the priority to be given differs from individual to individual and from situation to situation. Then, on what the priority must be given?

By giving some trouble to our mind for thinking in terms of whatever we get (viz. food, clothing, shelter, education, etc.) from the society, it will ultimately suggest that the first priority be given by every citizen should be for the cause of the society which they belong to.

Verily, Mismanagement comes whenever we start giving the first priority to one's self interest before the societal interest. After that people in the name of management will spend considerable amount of time and money in managing the effect (problem) rather than managing the cause. In other words, misdirected effort (energy) leads to mismanagement.

Insubordination of individual interest to societal interest is a manifestation of one's deep rooted belief and culture which can be nurtured only by "managing the belief"from an early age.

To recall an old saying, "Rome was not built

in a day", a belief for a good cause and a belief in the creation of good environment for our future generation cannot be inculcated in a day.

Nobody will stop us in forsaking our old myopic views and preparing to start a long journey from today onwards for a better tomorrow to be built on common belief of social benefits. If so, after 20 years we will be having a smooth landing in an era where everyone can afford to have a true smile from the heart of heart.

Presently, an unanswered question is lurking in my mind. Is a jumbo size ministry with its CEO (Chief Executive Officer) who professes survival of the fittest instead of collective survival, and who while talking of reducing government jobs increases the number of ministers thereby increasing extra expenditure and burdens the general public, a sign of good governance?

After all, our CEO is going to have another sunny day for expanding its never ending tendrils of the spectre of his mismanagement to create a menace of his magic.

7 We See the Things with the Mind and not with the Eyes!

In the year 2001
Manipur

Not a many years ago while returning home in a fully packed bus from Imphal, I heard a discussion between two persons; an elderly person and a physically challenged blind young boy.

The young boy was narrating a story of two persons, of which one is blind, sitting inside a closed room. The boy said that outside the door, suddenly, there was a sound and the normal person ran towards the door to see what was there outside whereas the blind man has already known that it was the sound of the wind. The blind boy concluded the story by saying that we see the things with the mind and not with the eyes.

That day, the story could not fully and logically convince my inner self as to whether the statement is true.

In our locality, there live two small girls, Meena and Shilla, who are friends and live next doors. Whenever Meena made any mistakes, her mother used to reprimand her and Meena used to cry aloud uttering that she would never do again. Women in the neighbourhoods thought that Meena was often seriously beaten by her mother and had already drawn the conclusion that Meena's mother was a child beater.

Through the gossiping of the women in the neighbourhoods and through mouth to mouth publicity, everybody started believing that Meena's mother was a child beater. One day Meena and Shilla were playing at Meena's place in front of the house. Suddenly Shilla was fallen and was crying with full of dust on her frock. Meena's mother came out and was consoling Shilla while uttering that her mother would be worried if she saw her with full of dust, tried to remove the dust from the frock with her hand. At that time, Shilla's mother was looking from the window of her house and saw that her daughter was crying and the hand of Meena's mother was seen to be moving again and again against the back of Shilla. She thought that Meena's mother not only beat Meena but also had started beating Shilla. Then Shilla's mother rushed towards Meena's house and without any word attacked Meena's mother.

Then, finally, I realized that people see the things with the mind and not with the eyes.

Our mind which sees the things is governed by what we believed. And what we believed is influenced by what we have learnt and what we have experienced in our life. On the basis of our belief many a times we do many things thinking that it will lead us to our objectives or goals. But often objectives that we have chosen and the activities we have undertaken are not related in any meaningful manner. It is similar to choosing our destination in the east and whatsoever the activities we do are instrumental to take us to the west.

Our level of understanding or our psychological level never try to go to the roots of the problem, rather we prefer to spend considerable amount of our time in fighting the fire instead of finding the root cause of the fire.

Whosoever are happy to be born and brought up in our state, have seen the true beauty of the state, have breath the air and have drank the water of the land would like to have a peaceful and harmonious environment where at least we could have a sound good night's sleep.

Amidst different organizations having different objectives and strengths of their own, it's the common people who suffer most. Those who can afford to move out of the state have already contemplated to leave the state. And the parents have already started instructing their children who are studying outside not to come back to their home state after their studies.

8 Is Humanity becoming an Endangered Species?

In the year 2002
Manipur

While growing up, when we started wobbling our legs, our concerned mother made a point that our tender legs should not be stepping onto ants that were crawling on the floor by telling us it would amount to sinning ourselves, if the ants got killed.

Whenever our tender hands tried to reach and catch an alluring butterfly sitting on the green leaves of a flower our mother stopped us by reminding us of getting sin if the butterfly got injury or killed.

For fear of getting sins we have learnt to love insects. In due course of time, we have learnt to love not only the insects but also the birds and animals and then we started rearing cats, dogs and different type of birds as pets.

Eventually, when one grows up into a man in such an environment of loving insects and animals, they approached to various institutions and agencies for funding the projects of protecting endangered species. Some of the projects often we heard of were tiger project, crocodile project, elephant project. etc.

What we observed was the protective nature of the parents on one side and on the other gradual toughening both mentally and physically of a child while preparing the child to step into the strange, competitive and violent environment where the child would be dwelling in the would be tomorrows.

This process of toughening started from an early age. Whenever the child was involved in squabbling, the parents would take the side of their wards and even encouraged the child to beat other harder, next time when the opportunity comes.

As and when the relative or uncles from the neighbourhood dropped in, the parents in their eagerness to show the agility and prow ness of their child to the visitors, asked the child to punch and kick just like Bruce Lee.

Sometimes, the child while demonstrating his skills ended up in punching and kicking the visiting uncles and every onlooker laughed, appreciated the child and encouraged the child with clapping.

Parents, particularly the father would never want his son to come back home beaten by the children of others.

Here, let me recall the story of a person. During his childhood, he grew up to be a peace loving, believing in making friends, had a fear of wrong doing or thinking ill of other. As a matter of fact, his value system was influenced by his early age of education in Seven day Adventist school.

One day, at the age of 13, while playing in the playground a boy of the same locality provoked him to fight with him. Since, he did not want other to consider him timid, reluctantly he started fighting with the boy who challenged him. Fortunately, the elder persons of locality separated them before any of them got injury.

When the boy returned home, his father who was already informed by the other about the fighting in the playground was waiting for him.

The boy's father told the boy that people were telling that the other boy had beaten him. The father, further, instructed the boy to go and break the head of the other boy, if not, told the boy not come back home.

The boy was in dilemma not knowing what to do. He looked for his mother to be on his side but not to be seen nearby. The boy had taken the father's words into his heart. He was really shocked and wondered why his father wanted him to become a hooligan when he was not that type.

The boy came out of the house, searching for the boy with whom he fought a short while ago. Luckily, he found the boy with some of his friends in the playground. The boy approached the other boy and told him to complete the fight which was stopped because of the interference of the elders.

The two boys were about to engaged in fight once again. But, that time, the boy's father who was following from a distance unknown to the boy, intervened them by telling that while living in the same locality one should not fight with each other.

The father's action might be to test the courage of his son or training him to become a tough man. Whatever might be the case, from that day onwards, even at the slightest provocation he was drawn into fight or squabble with the other. Many a times he did wonder why he could not restrain himself, whenever he thought injustice being done to him or to other.

Often chances are high that those who have grown up in such environment are not likely to cultivate the love for other but may be influential in nurturing the hatred for other. Subsequently, a violent environment of the future where people will have no mutual respect and trust among themselves is in the process of seeding. If steps are not taken up at the right time, one day it would become very difficult for Manipuri to live in Manipur. Seemingly, most of the parents have forgotten to teach the love for mankind to their children who are supposed to be the pillars of our future society.

Nevertheless, there are few persons who have grown up in loving environments of home and its neighbourhood, who have imbibed strong values from their parents and other institutions/ schools, colleges and universities. They do have a concern for other and society. To them society comes first. They dream, think, do and live for the betterment of the society which gives them the identity of their existence. They have sympathy, kindness and understanding of mankind. They have a system of beliefs that concentrates on common human need and seeks way of solving human problems based on reason rather than faith in God. Perhaps, this system of beliefs is the precious endangered species called humanity.

It will be surprise to know that it is because of this few people having humanity, we are still able to hold together and able to exist together as Manipur and Manipuri. Majority of us are happy that they are still alive and working for the cause of the state to bring peace, harmony and cohesive society while other few groups are still creating hurdles to the works of this few people.

Sometimes we do worry about what will be happening to our future when this few people get extinct along with their humanity due to changing waves of time. I have a fear that if their beliefs are frequently exposed to counter propaganda and today's environment of daily bloodshed, the humanity in them will not last longer.

Is not a time has come for us to approach the financial institution for fund to protect this endangered species called humanity from the state?

With the fund we get, we can build a cluster village for this endangered species. We can make a survey and gather the people with humanity from each district of the state and bring them to this village to settle down. If it is so, our state will be in the map of world tourism.

People from different parts of the world would be visiting the village where we have protected and kept the endangered species. People would be eager to see the endangered species. The tourist guide would be pointing to a particular cottage in the village and with a pride, telling the tourist, "here lives the endangered humanity from Imphal east", and pointing to another cottage, the guide would say "here lives the endangered species from Ukrul", and so on.

If this is feasible, our state will be financially better off with its growth in tourism and would complement a lot to state's crutched salary base economy.

9 An Efficient but not an Effective Manager

In the year 2002
Manipur

Every industry taken up in Manipur with lots of hopes and expectations seems to disappear shortly after its establishment. Almost all the public undertakings except one or two which are fighting for survival other have no longer found to exist today.

In contrast to the situation of public undertakings, some of the private organisations are doing roaring business and we can learn a lesson or two from them how to run a business enterprise in Manipur.

At the beginning of 1990s, an undertaking of central government called Manipur State Drugs and Pharmaceutical Limited was established with the equity participation between central and state government.

At that time, people had a high hope that with establishment of this pharmaceutical company, there will be no ailments in the state and the state will be marching towards a healthy society.

At the beginning, for the manufacturing of medicines from bulk drugs, the management of the company hired a production manager from Hindustan Antibiotic Limited, Pune.

The production manager manufactured all the medicines he used to manufacture at HAL, Pune.

But only two or three products are found to have its market in Manipur. Since the geographical and climatic conditions of Manipur are unique on its own, the common disease prevailing in Manipur and in and around Pune must also be different.

Common sense tells that before deciding which type of medicine to be produced, the management of the company should have at least consulted the doctors of the state regarding the type of medicines and its composition and for what type of ailments that may find its market in Manipur and nearby states.

The unsold medicines have a shelf life span of two years. Because of the high transportation cost the products cannot be transported to other places where it may find its market. After the expiry dates, all the medicines are disposed off. Since then the company become sick and no longer found to exist today. The production manager was indeed efficient in manufacturing the medicines but not effective in the choice of medicines.

10 Managing Belief of Employees

An organisation comes into existence with certain objectives to be accomplished. Without management, Business organisation will be a mere collection of man, material, financial resources etc., incapable of achieving anything. It is the management which utilises the resources of the organization to accomplish its objectives effectively and efficiently.

For increasing the efficiency of the organisation, management looks for increasing the efficiency of the employees who handle the other resources of the organisation. And different ways of managing people have emerged over the years.

In the words of Peter Drucker in respect of the managing people "in the fast changing world, what worked yesterday probably doesn't work today. Way back, the right way was top down control-centralisation, latter decentralisation came into vogue. Today the team approach is considered to be ideal".

Again in today's fast ever changing environment, organisation tends to become lean due to downsizing of its employees. So the management of the organisation has to increase the efficiency of the limited no. of employees in a team approach to increase the productivity of the organisation.

Moreover, in today's work environment, increasingly there are educated workers. Educated employees/workers cannot be managed as subordinates the way it used to be. Employees have to be managed as associates/partners. The very definition of partnership is that all partners are equal. It is also the definition of the partnership that partners cannot be ordered. They have to be persuaded.

As the importance of managing people for the successfully running the organisation increases, various management experts have developed various approaches to managing people over the years.

Fredric W. Taylor introduced differential rating system, a system which advocates paying of more pay for productive workers and less pay for less productive workers.

Robert Owen believed that by providing

better working conditions and social environment, people will be motivated to work. But behavioural scientist believed that an individual is motivated to work for many reasons in addition to making money and forming social relationship.

Chris Argyris keeping into consideration of the employees' need for self reliance and accomplishment, favours allowing subordinates much more independence and decision making power, and creating more informal organisation structure.

McGregor suggested two ways of managing people in his theory X and theory Y. Theory X assumes that people don't want to work, so they must be forced and controlled. Theory Y assumes that they really do want to work and require proper motivation.

Abraham Maslow views that different people requires different ways of managing them.

But the most striking revelation is the finding of the experiment conducted at the Hawthorne plant of Western Eletric Company, near Chicago. The studies revealed that the powerful incentives towards increased production was not due to physical working conditions or financial rewards but was the result of Hawthorne effect. The phenomenon in which the employees would work harder if they believed management was concerned about their welfare and the supervisor paid special attention to them is called Hawthorne effect.

In today's context when the management of the organisation is focussing on lean organisation and team approach, the relevancy of the findings of the Hawthorne experiment has become more prominent.

The increasing demand of transparency in corporate governance will also contribute in the efforts of the management to create the right type of environment for igniting the team spirit.

Keeping in view of the emerging scenario of focusing on lean organisation, team approach and transparency in the governance, managing the belief of the employees for the smooth functioning and achieving the organisation's objectives become more prominent.

Increasingly management of the people is a marketing job. And in marketing one does not begin with the question, what do we want? One begins with the question; what does the other party want? What are its values? What are its goals? What does it consider results?

Moreover, managing the organisation now involves aligning the employees' goal with those of the organisational goal.

In the organisation, the formal linking thread among the members of the organisation is the formal authority-responsibility relationship. But this alone cannot ensure the much needed team spirit for achieving optimal efficiency of the organisation.

The other linking thread which is informal in nature is the belief and trust between supervisor and subordinates as well as among the peers.

The team spirit leading to organisational efficiency can be induced if the formal authority responsibility relationship is synergised by the informal linking thread of trust and belief.

One's belief and one's behaviour are highly correlated. A belief is a descriptive thought that a person holds about something.

Many a times, management of the organisation found out that employees/subordinates do not behave the way as they are expected. But for the management, it is imperative that employees/ subordinates must behave the way as they are expected and their behaviour direct towards the goal of the organisation.

If the employees have beliefs and values that conform to the belief and values of the managements or with the culture of the organisation, employees behaviours will be as per it is expected and will be directed towards the objectives of the organisation. Here lies the importance of managing belief of the employees in the organisation.

For inculcating gradually in the minds of the employees the right type of beliefs and values for inducing team spirit and ensuring goal directed behaviours, the following procedure can be considered:

Stage 1. Management should clearly identify and define the corporate values & beliefs.

Stage 2. Understanding the employees' present values and beliefs

Stage 3. Analysing the gap between the corporate values and the individual values. And determine what aspects of the values to be inculcated in the minds of the employees.

Stage 4. Identifying the activities through which the needed aspects of values and belief to be inculcated.

Stage 5. Execution of the activities.

Stage 6. Establish an effective communication channel between management and employees in order that individual/ groups could identify with the corporate objectives.

In short, in today's fast ever changing environment, when the organisations are focusing on lean, team approach and transparency, managing the belief of the employees so as to ingrain the beliefs and values of the organisation in the minds of employees in order to induce the desired goal directed behaviour has its relevance.

In other words, tuning beliefs of employees into the organisational values is an imperative for the success of any organisation.

11 Conclusion

It is through education that we have seen the unfolding of changes in the society. In today's context we are giving importance to the formal education and keeping in view of the type of transformation that we would like to bring in the student, the curriculum of the courses is being framed and the right type of environment is created.

If we want that our future generations should be competitive and focus on individual achievement then accordingly curriculum could be made. And if, what we require today are good citizens who should have the societal concern as the first priority and then individual achievement then accordingly we can frame the course curriculum.

In short, the need of the society, education policy and the activities through which this policy are implemented should be correlated and consistent. Otherwise, it will be similar to setting the objective of going to the east but the every step we make take us to the west.

Before and by the time when this article "Who is to be blamed?" was written in the Feb. Month of 2000, in the rural areas of the state and in some places of the urban areas, mass copying in the examinations was a regular phenomenon. Parents and the teachers also took important roles in helping the students to copy. And that was one of the saddest things in my life.

But today, nobody copies in any examinations conducted in Manipur after some voluntary organisations and revolutionary activists have taken up the matter.

At the background when the peoples have started demanding of quality education, administrators of educational institutions and teachers should be very careful about the term "quality". The term should be clearly defined and stated in the measurable or conceivable parameters. Otherwise one day schools, colleges and universities will be blamed for giving the students degrees but not making them learn the values of life so as to become beautiful human beings.

In *Rigveda*, it is mentioned," Education is a force which makes an individual self reliant as well selfless". Whether one agrees to the statement or not, the saying will remain for a long time to come.

For having a cohesive society and for a better tomorrow we need feasible and implement able ideas of the intellectual members of the society and not a mere imagination of a few people that will be detrimental to the society or which cannot be implemented.

Has not the right time arrived for the intellectuals of the society to gather their courage to speak out and shoulder their responsibility as expected of them?

Smile plays a very important role in our day to day life in making our life meaningful and it is a magic particularly at work place. One should not leave the smile behind in the closet when they go to their work place. The smile which is being referred to is the true smile from the heart but not the deceiving smile to deceive other.

Smile gives a warm feeling to other and makes them comfortable while they are with you even for a moment and that moment will linger in their mind for a long time and may be instrumental in having many well wishers of yours.

Is it not our responsibility being a citizen of the state to create the right type of environment where everybody bears a true smile on their face?

While believing that culture is handed down from generation to generation, we should try to protect the core belief which forms the core identity of the culture. Any sort of behaviour of a few people which are going to affect our society should be nipped in the bud before it becomes a part of the culture of our society. If not, our culture may be misinterpreted by other and we may lose our identity.

And without the identity of our own, where will be our existence?

If an environment suffocates not only a few of us but also the others; should we change it, adapt to it or leave the environment?

Whatsoever the answer may be, those who are courageous and having the concern for other will strive to change the environment for a better tomorrow.

Custodians of the society, particularly those who shoulder the bigger responsibility should profess collective survival and inculcate in the minds of people the feeling of unity to bring a cohesive society.

Bad governance or misadministration occurs only when we lose our focus on the right type of priorities to be emphasised. The turmoiled environment that we are witnessing today is the reflection and indication of wrong priorities of the governance. What should be the priority of the society and its people should be ingrained in the minds of the people right from the school days, only then one day when they shoulder the responsibility of the society, they can visualise the right type of priority for the society.

But it seems the framers of the curriculum of the schools have forgotten to include even a little dose of patriotism into the curriculum not to mention about the inclusion of the importance of our identity and its existence.

In today's context, do we still have the pride of being a Manipuri?

Whatsoever the answer may be, I believe a time has come for all of us to act for the cause of Manipuri identity.

Index

❑❑❑